From the lonely Eileen Doyle

13/10/13

GW00676420

50 Great Lessons from Life

TONY SPOLLEN

OAK·TREE·PRESS

Published by OAK TREE PRESS
19 Rutland Street, Cork, Ireland
www.oaktreepress.com

© 2013 Tony Spollen

A catalogue record of this book is available from the British Library.

ISBN 978 1 78119 073 9 (Hardback)
ISBN 978 1 78119 074 6 (ePub)
ISBN 978 1 78119 075 3(Kindle)

All rights reserved.
No part of this publication may be reproduced or transmitted in
any form or by any means, including photocopying, recording or
electronically without written permission of the publisher.
Such written permission also must be obtained before any part of
this publication is stored in a retrieval system of any nature.
Requests for permission should be directed to Oak Tree Press,
19 Rutland Street, Cork, Ireland or info@oaktreepress.com.

Printed in Ireland by SPRINT-print Limited

CONTENTS

FOREWORD

In this hectic world that we live in, we are all bombarded with suggestions on how to improve one's life. Some are aspirational, some are fanciful, some are basic and mostly, they are one size fits all. One thing's for sure, there are a myriad of lessons to live one's life – and trying to decipher them is difficult. That's why Tony's book is so special – he takes it all and lays it out in such an easy manner. It is beautiful in its simplicity, its brevity and its verity.

I have had the privilege of knowing Tony for many years and this book is testimony to his straightforward, sensible and warm, embracing attitude to life. His generosity in sharing his thoughts is a gift that we can all enjoy. And importantly, we can and should pass it down through the generations as what he writes is timeless. I hope that you enjoy reading *50 Great Lessons from Life* as much as my family and I did.

Tony O'Reilly Jnr.
Dublin
May 2013

INTRODUCTION

At the age of 65, it seemed a good time to write some lessons from my life's experiences that could be of help to my four children.

Many ideas came to mind and the number of lessons grew.

So too did the time it took to make them short.

One year later, there were 50.

That's how this book came into being.

My sincere wish is that it will help you to improve your life.

Tony Spollen
Dublin
May 2013

1 You can feel good immediately

A friend of mine, who was a great public speaker, was about to address a large audience in Dublin.

The room was full and very noisy.

However, as soon as he stood at the podium, there was silence.

He had that ability to control the room and to create a sense of occasion.

As he faced the audience, he was breathing in a slow and shallow way through his nose. This kept him calm. It was a technique he had learnt many years ago.

For an hour, they were spellbound.

When the clapping finally stopped, he thanked them and walked to the car park.

Once there, however, his worries surfaced.

One negative thought came into his head and this attracted another and then another. He felt so down.

Then something amazing happened.

Shortly after leaving the car park, he stopped at a traffic light to buy a newspaper and asked the elderly newspaper seller, who was standing in the rain, how he was.

"Have never been better. I have my health. What more do I need?" was his reply.

This was from someone with few material possessions, who was getting wet and earning very little and yet was really happy.

And each day, as my friend bought his newspaper, the newspaper seller's response was always the same: "Couldn't be better".

My friend realised then that he could be happy again.

The newspaper seller taught him that, if you have your health and decide to make each moment the best, you will feel good immediately.

That simple lesson changed his life.

2 Three priceless assets make you very wealthy

You are a very wealthy person.

You may not feel that way, particularly in these times of recession.

Perhaps that's because you have always thought of wealth in terms of material possessions.

But money, property and investments are the small part of wealth.

Your real wealth is in your 'big balance sheet of life'.

That 'big balance sheet' holds your three priceless assets:

- Your ability to make each moment the best;
- Your health;
- Your sense of humour.

The 'little balance sheet' holds your material possessions:

- Money;
- Property;
- Investments.

Your big balance sheet has made you very wealthy.

Keep it strong and you will have almost everything that you need.

3 Your health is more valuable than gold

It was a Sunday evening when the phone rang.

The caller sounded energetic and enthusiastic and full of life – as he always did.

But he had huge pressures.

He was suffering from cancer.

"How do you see the banking situation?" he asked.

We had a long discussion, and he thanked me for my thoughts.

Within a few months, he was dead.

Brian Lenihan was brilliant, hard-working, pleasant and had a great sense of humour.

Even though his background was in law, he became Ireland's Minister for Finance at a time of enormous economic problems, both at home and abroad.

He faced his illness with courage.

He tried to stay strong.

Following chemotherapy, he would go to the Irish Parliament to answer questions, asking his political opponents to ignore his medical condition.

It is hard to be strong when your health suffers.

With good health, you have almost everything.

With poor health, life is tough.

4   Your mind can make your life great

Breathe in a slow and shallow way through your nose. This technique will help you to be calm in times of great challenge.

Then, decide to make each moment the best.

Soon, all negative thoughts will leave your mind.

It will be like poison draining from your system.

Your mind then will be clear and your energy will return.

At times in the past, it may have seemed that everything was going wrong for you at the same time.

This was because one negative thought entered your mind and attracted more negatives – and soon you were on overload.

When this happens, scenarios with bad endings start to play out in your mind and you become worried.

Those negative thoughts and worries are like poison.

They damage your health.

You can stop both negative thoughts and worry immediately by getting your breathing right and by deciding to make each moment the best.

Your mind can make your life great.

Be sure that it does.

5 You can eliminate worry

There is nothing to be said for worry.

And most of the things that people worry about never come to pass.

Worry has ruined and continues to ruin the lives of many people all over the world.

See it as poison.

Don't let it near you.

It is a danger to your health.

Many people spend much time worrying and suffer greatly.

As you breathe in a slow and shallow way though your nose and make each moment the best, you fill your system with goodness.

Then there is no room for worry.

When you make each moment the best, you will eliminate worry forever.

6 You can deal with tough challenges

When you eliminate worry and negative thoughts from your mind, create space.

Do nothing for a while.

Enjoy the feeling of badness draining from your system.

Flood your mind with goodness as you breathe well and make each moment the best.

While you will still have challenges, when you feel good, your thinking will be clear and you will be able to deal with them.

Your positive attitude will attract more positives.

Solutions will begin to emerge.

Trust in yourself.

Each one of us feels that our challenges are big.

But, in the overall scheme of things, they are tiny.

Five years ago, Simon Brown, a soldier with the British army in Iraq, was badly injured.

He lost the sight in one eye and has very limited vision in the other.

At first, he felt sorry for himself. But then he thought about his comrades who had died.

He returned to study and is now a teacher.

7 All things pass away

While out walking on a cold winter's night, a man wearing a hat approached me.

He didn't look well but seemed pleased to see me.

"How are you?" he asked.

It then dawned on me who he was.

The last time we had met was six months earlier, when he had been in great form.

He had been spending a lot of time at his Spanish villa and also in Paris, where he had an apartment. He was so happy and so healthy then.

It was hard to believe that this frail man was the same person.

Recently, he had been treated for a brain tumour and now was recovering.

He wanted to talk, so we went to my home which was nearby.

It seemed to me that evening that much of his old spark was still there and he himself said how lucky he was to have a second chance at life.

However, a short time after that, he died.

Material possessions, of which my friend had many, are tiny when compared to health.

Sometimes, it takes a small illness to realise this and make you adjust your priorities.

Sometimes, with a serious illness, it is too late.

8 Wish others well – but don't wish to be them

One day, a friend and I discussed old times and laughed a lot.

Suddenly, the conversation took a surprising turn.

He became very serious and said, "Life can be hard".

This surprised me, as he had good health and always seemed in great form.

He had a successful business, a big house and much money.

However, inside, he was sad and unhappy.

He told me of his son's bad health and how he would gladly give away everything if it would make his son well again.

He felt helpless.

He had discovered that real wealth has nothing to do with material possessions.

It is, he said, "all about health".

As you go through life, you will realise more and more that, very often, things are not what they seem.

Keep breathing well, making each moment the best and be grateful for the life you have.

9 Create a positive atmosphere

There is a restaurant in America where the waiters pay to work.

Where else in the world would this happen?

The owner found a property in a great location, furnished it beautifully and employed top class chefs.

The restaurant's reputation grew and it became very popular.

At staff meetings, the owner encouraged everyone to express their ideas.

They decided to rent the tables to waiters, feeling that waiters relying solely on 'tips' would work really hard.

The diners were impressed with the service and were generous.

Out of those tips, the waiters paid their table rental.

The service got better and better.

The customers, the owners, the waiters and the suppliers were happy.

And, as the business grew, the whole area benefitted.

In the restaurant's accounts, waiters appeared as an 'income' item and not a 'cost'.

A friend of mine also built a successful business using a simple formula: he delivered his product ahead of the promised time, paid his suppliers ahead of the agreed time, paid his staff well and gave them generous leave.

This all helped to create a wonderful atmosphere.

The customers, the suppliers and the staff were positive and wanted the business to do better and better.

My friend did not set out to make a lot of money but his positive approach made him a fortune.

When you set a positive tone, much can be achieved.

10   Everyone is insecure

Provence is a lovely part of France, where many wealthy people live.

One evening, a businessman who had recently bought a property in the area arrived late for a dinner that was being hosted by someone who had lived there for many years.

His flight had been delayed. He was irritated and made a noisy entrance, complaining about "that inefficient airline".

Those attending the dinner were used to private jets and chauffeur-driven cars.

This show of insecurity was unnecessary.

A more secure man would have said, "I am sorry for being late" and left it at that.

Loud and argumentative people are often very insecure. They crave recognition and need to feel important.

You can be certain that, at any function, whether business or social or whatever, everyone is insecure. It is only a question of degree.

11 You will never really know anyone

A well-dressed and well-spoken man sat at a table in a famous restaurant in London.

He looked relaxed and comfortable.

He ordered expensive food and wine and was treated well by the waiters, who were anticipating a big tip.

Throughout the evening, he was courteous and pleasant.

Then, as he finished his brandy, he took off his jacket, rolled up his shirt sleeves and asked to be escorted to the kitchen.

He had no money – nor any embarrassment.

We often judge people by their appearance, or by the way they speak.

A good poker player exudes confidence without a single good card in his hand.

He never shows the weakness of his position.

World champion snooker player Denis Taylor said that, as he played his final shot in the championship, he was shaking and could hardly hold his cue.

He hid his nervousness well.

We sometimes judge the book by the cover and are disappointed.

We sometimes judge the bottle of wine by the label, and again are disappointed.

Does anyone really know you? Nobody does!

You will never really know anyone.

Everyone has greater strengths, greater weaknesses and greater challenges than you realise.

Don't rush to judgement.

You are certainly wrong.

It's only a question of how wrong.

12 Ignore slights

Don't let little things bother you.

Don't get irritated or upset if:

- Your phone call is not answered or returned;
- You are kept waiting;
- You are not included in a meeting or event;
- You appear to be ignored;
- You are placed down the pecking order at a function.

Think on a higher level.

Don't read too much into the situation.

Most people are pre-occupied with their own issues and are not trying to hurt you or be mean to you.

There is usually a simple explanation.

Many slights are unintentional. Most are imagined.

When you think on a higher level, you are in control.

13 You have no reason to feel sorry for yourself

The elderly newspaper seller makes each moment the best.

His instant response is: "Things couldn't be better. I have my health. What more do I need?"

He realises how lucky he is.

He loves life, enjoys a laugh and makes everyone he meets feel good.

But, for many others, life is tough.

Each day, on our TV screens, we see scenes of violence from around the world.

If you walk down any street, you see people who are suffering.

They are sad and there is a sense of hopelessness in their expressions.

Often, they have nobody to turn to.

Although you may have big issues to face, with a clear head you will deal with them well.

When you consider the great things in your life, starting with your three priceless assets, you will realise how fortunate you are.

When you decide to make each moment the best, mind your health and maintain a good sense of humour, you need little else.

The elderly newspaper seller understands this well.

14 'Smell the roses' as often as you can

Summer in the West of Ireland can be magical.

One day, a middle-aged man sat by a lake.

He had big challenges.

But his breathing was great and he decided to make each moment the best.

In that wonderful setting he watched the warm breeze skim the surface of that lake and the ripples as they crept to the bank.

The clear blue sky and the green fields and forests and mountains created a sense of calmness and timelessness.

It was as if life was standing still.

He remembered a poem from his schooldays:

> *Four ducks on a pond*
> *A green bank beyond*
> *A blue sky of spring*
> *Birds on the wing*
> *Oh what a sight*
> *To remember for years*
> *To remember with tears!*

He had been so lucky.

Where had those 50 years gone?

And yet, in the timeless world of nature, little had changed.

Having enjoyed a great day, he decided to slow down.

When you create space and take time to smell the roses, you feel the magic of the moment.

This is your life, and it is a good life.

15 Forgive all

Most people whom we meet are kind and helpful.

Only a few have been unkind and unhelpful.

Forgive them!

It is over!

Don't let anger and hurt stay in your system.

Let them go.

Be kind to those who you forgive.

Once you forgive, your health will improve.

Don't harbour any bad feelings or grudges.

They make you old.

Then, as you move at a slower pace, remember that everyone has much bigger challenges than appear on the surface.

Make allowances. Most people are doing their best.

Like you, they have made many mistakes and have many regrets.

They are human, too.

16 Be big and generous

Bill Shankley, the legendary manager of Liverpool Football Club, whose team had just beaten Newcastle United in the FA Cup Final, went over to the Newcastle players as the game ended, consoling them and telling them that their day would come.

This was the act of a big and generous person, who knew how awful players feel when they lose an important game.

When you are big and generous, you and those around you feel better.

When you are big and generous, you make people feel valued.

You make them feel important.

You listen to their views and you share some of what you have learnt.

You laugh at jokes, even though you have heard them many times.

Big and generous people don't have to win every game or debate.

They know that a positive atmosphere brings out the best in everyone.

So they create a positive atmosphere wherever they are.

17 Write kind and thoughtful notes

The former Chairman of the AIB Group, Niall Crowley was a big and generous man.

After each Audit Committee meeting, he would send me a hand-written note, thanking me for my work.

These short notes were read many times.

They meant so much.

They were so appreciated; they were so motivational.

A note that says "Well done" or "Thank you" or "Good luck" or "I'm sorry" can make someone feel great.

When you write such notes, you will be amazed at how well they will be received.

It won't be forgotten – even after many years.

Most people receive few such notes in their lifetime.

It is surprising that something that takes such little time and is so appreciated is so rare.

18 Life is a marathon, not a sprint

A marathon runner looks calm and serene as he runs that long race.

He has his challenges.

Conditions are not always easy.

But he will enjoy the run and will stay the course.

Pace yourself. Avoid rushing and strain.

Stay positive.

You will overcome your challenges.

Take everything in your stride.

Sometimes, you will need to change pace.

Do it gently.

Stay in control.

Continue to make each moment the best.

19   Think young and stay young

When you eliminate worry, your energy will return.

That energy will help to keep you young.

When you feel like this, you find good in others and the world seems brighter and your challenges seem smaller.

Try to 'smell the roses' in silence and in solitude as often as you can.

That sense of calm and beauty and timelessness also will help you to stay young.

When you feel happy and healthy and big, you feel young.

A good sense of humour and laughter also will keep you young.

Don't see yourself as getting old.

Think young and you will be young.

20 Whether you win or lose, have fun

Some years ago, a French golfer, Jan Van deVelde, was leading the British Open golf championship as he came to the last hole at Carnoustie, in Scotland.

He could afford to take a 6 on that par 4 hole and still win.

He knew that to win the British Open is one of the great achievements in golf.

He wanted to win it so badly that he became his own toughest opponent (many people experience this).

The pressure got to him.

As the tension built, he rushed his shots – to get them over with – and made mistakes.

These mistakes increased his tension.

Things went from bad to worse.

He lost the championship.

This pattern is common.

Everyone likes to win.

But you won't always win – nobody does.

Continue to believe in yourself and relax.

And remember it is only a game.

Should tension creep in, concentrate.

Concentration relieves tension.

If you lose, it will not be the end of the world.

Whether you win or lose, have fun.

21 Go for it

Fear of failure, more than anything else, holds people back from achieving.

If you are afraid of failing, you may never get started.

You should see mistakes as part of life's experience. Everyone makes mistakes.

When a wealthy man was asked how he had made so much money, he said that it was probably because he had made more mistakes than most other people.

The great entrepreneurs and great companies of the world make many mistakes.

Many success stories are the result of trying, failing, trying again and then finally succeeding.

Pharmaceutical companies try to discover cures for illnesses; their experiments fail; and then they have successes.

Great sportsmen suffer many defeats and then break through to win.

If you really want something, go for it.

Stop thinking about going for it.

Don't be afraid to fail.

If you fail, learn the lessons and start again.

This is what many of the great achievers have done.

22 People need to feel important

Many surveys show that a person's need to feel important is greater than their need to be loved.

At 5-star hotels, guests pay a lot and are treated very well.

On their arrival, the head porter greets them like long-lost friends.

He makes them feel welcome and important.

Someone brings them to their magnificent room where everything is perfect.

As they go to dinner, the head waiter greets them and he too makes them feel so important: "Your usual table …", "Your usual drink…", "So nice to see you again".

Top class executives recognise that people need to feel important and valued.

People glow with pride when they receive an award.

They feel important.

Every person is important. Make them feel that way.

23 Help and encourage

We all need help and encouragement at different times.

As we began life, we had our parents, then our teachers and family members, then team-mates, then business colleagues and bosses and mentors.

All helped and encouraged us in some way.

Many influenced us greatly.

Those who were there for us in tough times are never forgotten.

Try to help others who are going through tough times.

They may feel alone.

When you help someone, you often have a friend for life.

When you encourage someone and see them grow and develop, you get great satisfaction.

Be there for people when you can. You will not regret it.

There are many who need help and encouragement.

24 Listen

You can learn so much by listening, yet very few people are good listeners.

You will learn nothing by talking, yet many people talk a lot.

Why do they talk so much?

Is it a need to feel important?

Is it a lack of interest in what others have to say?

Many professional interviewers seem to have a problem listening, often interrupting.

They have a huge need to talk.

Listening is a skill.

It requires much practice.

Try to listen without interrupting.

At first, you may find this very difficult.

Once you practice, you will get better.

You will be amazed at how much more you will learn when you become a good listener.

25 Silence can be powerful

Many people find it hard to stay silent.

They rush to fill the gap when there is a lull in the conversation.

By listening and by staying silent, you give yourself big advantages.

A famous American businessman – a great listener, who had the ability to stay silent – often would sit at meetings for hours saying nothing.

His silence conveyed knowledge, self-confidence, power and maturity and this helped to earn him many millions of dollars.

He learnt so much.

26 Create space

When someone wants a meeting, often the matter can be dealt with in a phone call.

Don't let unnecessary meetings use up your space.

If you avoid meetings where possible and encourage short reports, you will free up much space in your life.

By picking the right people and delegating well, you will create more space.

That ability to create space is a great skill – one you should develop.

Many senior people, despite greater responsibilities, have more time than middle managers.

They have learnt to create space.

Having created space, breathe well and make each moment the best.

Sit with a blank pad and a clear head and you will be creative and of greater value to yourself and others.

27 Look and act the part

You often see the TV cameras zoom in on a President or a Prime Minister as they come down the steps of the plane, or cross the room, or move to the lectern.

You see someone who moves calmly in a well-cut dark suit and an immaculate white shirt.

There is no sense of rush.

There is a feeling of time, space and self-confidence.

They look the part and they act the part.

They expect things to run smoothly.

Learn from these senior people.

Because, each day, you market yourself.

So, be well-dressed and well-groomed and move at a dignified pace.

Always remember that when someone meets you for the first time they will form a view of you within five seconds.

It takes a lot to change that view.

Look the part – and act the part.

28 Be relaxed

You will be more effective and happier when you are relaxed.

As you continue to breathe in a slow and shallow way through your nose and make each moment the best, you are filling your system with goodness.

If you sit comfortably, close your eyes and do this exercise, you will feel relaxed and calm:

- Picture your forehead being relaxed, then your eyes and then the rest of your face.
- Move slowly down from your neck to your feet – all relaxed.
- Then start with your feet and move slowly to your forehead – all relaxed.
- Soon, you will feel warm and calm.
- Keep breathing well.
- If a thought enters your mind or you hear a noise, say to yourself, "Relax".
- Then, starting with your forehead, repeat the process.
- Soon, you will feel drowsy and you will have a short sleep.
- As you wake, count from 10 to zero and stretch gently.

29 Quit when you are ahead

Today people everywhere feel stupid for failing to anticipate the world-wide recession.

With the benefit of hindsight, the situation that developed should have been obvious.

But few, even those with much business experience and access to expert advice, saw the economic problems that were coming.

So don't be hard on yourself.

You are human. You won't get it right all the time. Nobody does.

Many in Ireland, who had seen significant growth in asset values in the previous decade, saw those values drop sharply.

In the past, wise investors believed in 'leaving a little for the next person' and they quit when they were ahead.

There will be new opportunities in the future and again there will be the chance to quit when ahead.

But always keep in perspective success in the area of material possessions: investments, property and cash are tiny when compared to your priceless assets:

- Your ability to make each moment the best;
- Your health;

- Your sense of humour.

30 'Home ground' is always an advantage

Whether it is a sporting occasion, a business occasion or a social function, home ground is always an advantage.

You are more in control.

You know the surroundings well.

There are no surprises.

It is your show.

You can organise things as you wish.

You eliminate much uncertainty.

You are more comfortable, more relaxed, and more confident.

Make 'home ground' your preferred choice.

31 Learn to speak in public

The father of the bride was dreading his speech. He hadn't slept well for weeks.

As he stood in front of relations and friends, he froze – then rushed to get it over with.

He tried to tell jokes.

He was embarrassed.

But the guests were sympathetic. Few would have wished to speak themselves.

Many surveys show that speaking in public ranks very high in people's fears – higher even than the fear of nuclear war or of death.

Speaking in public takes practice.

If you practice, you will overcome your fear and you will learn to speak well.

The ability to speak well will boost your confidence.

It also will enhance your image as a leader.

Good speakers prepare well.

It is a performance.

They look and feel the part.

They check the room and practice there, to become comfortable with the microphone, the temperature and the general lay-out.

They get their pace right (this takes much practice).

They use stories more than statistics.

They avoid notes.

They connect with their audience and the really good ones have that great ability to create a sense of occasion.

32 Communicate in a simple and clear way

For those who heard John Kennedy's inaugural address as President of America or his speech at the Brandenburg Gate in Berlin, when he said, "Ich bin ein Berliner", the memory will always be there.

When President Reagan spoke at the Brandenburg Gate 25 years later and said, "Mr Gorbachev, tear down that wall", that too was memorable.

Great speakers look the part, act the part and connect with their audience.

They create a sense of occasion.

Good writers, too, connect with their readers and make each sentence interesting.

Their readers become engrossed; they find it hard to put the book down.

When speaking, avoid rambling … when writing, avoid padding.

If you make things simple, clear and enjoyable, it will help to keep your audience interested from beginning to end.

It is surprising that, in a world of instant communications, good communicators are so rare.

33 Don't mistake kindness for weakness

The CEO of a large group asked the newly-appointed Marketing Manager to make a presentation to the Group Board.

The CEO's advice was to be well-prepared.

He reminded his colleague, "Today, you will be presenting to very senior people, who are very strong and well capable of taking tough decisions. They will be kind and fair – but don't mistake that kindness for weakness".

Standing at the podium to address the distinguished and successful Board members, the Marketing Manager felt tense.

He knew that it was important to make his presentation simple, clear and short.

It had taken him much time to prepare – and it showed.

The Directors were appreciative.

When the presentation was over, many made kind comments.

The Chairman thanked him and congratulated him.

As the Marketing Manager was leaving the boardroom, pleased with his performance and the Board's reaction, the conversation turned to the next item on the agenda.

"Closure of the Dublin plant at the end of this month", said the Chairman. "We heard the Finance Director's arguments earlier. It is necessary for the good of the company. Anyone disagree?"

With hardly a moment's pause, he continued, "No? Good, please minute the Board's decision, Mr. Secretary. Next item, please".

In less than a minute, 500 people had lost their jobs, and a once-proud part of the company was closed forever.

The Marketing Manager remembered the Chairman's words: "Don't mistake their kindness for weakness".

The Board had been kind and fair to the Marketing Manager.

He had felt the power of their kindness. He also knew that it hid no weakness when tough decisions were called for.

It was a great lesson. A lesson he never forgot.

34 Don't be the person to give bad news

A friend of mine was watching a soccer match on TV when the doorbell rang.

It was his neighbour, who looked uncomfortable.

"Unfortunately, someone has smashed the windscreen of your car", he said.

While his neighbour had done him a favour by reporting the damage, my friend was in no mood to be grateful.

He had been given bad news.

At such times, there is an urge to 'shoot the messenger' – to blame the person who gave the bad news.

If his neighbour had said, "I am glad they didn't steal your car" or "In comparison to another neighbour who has cancer, it's not such a big problem", it might have made things easier.

My friend did his best to be gracious, but he didn't do well.

Try not to be the person to give bad news.

35 Be slow to confide

Be slow to confide.

And confide in few.

Many see information as power; some like to share it to show how important they are.

Someone who is your friend today may not be your friend tomorrow, and it is dangerous to assume continued loyalty and confidentiality.

Be careful when taking a drink, because it is often then that someone shares a confidence and regrets it later.

You have no need to show how 'in the loop' you are.

When someone trusts you with a confidence, don't let them down.

Maintain confidences.

Listen more .

Talk less.

36 Pick the right people and delegate

The Captain spent much time on the bridge.

He knew that he had good people in charge of all areas of the ship.

He had confidence in his people. He also delegated well.

He knew every member of the crew and he made each one feel important and valued.

They, in turn, respected him and trusted him.

He always gave credit for a successful voyage to his crew and praised them a lot.

Those more senior in the Group did not see him as a threat and those reporting to him loved working for him.

The atmosphere on the ship was always positive and the owners, passengers and the crew all benefitted from this.

When he was made CEO of the Group nobody, apart from himself, was surprised.

In his new role, he made sure that all who reported to him were better than him in their own particular area of expertise and he gave credit for success to both the Board and the staff.

It served him well and it served the organisation well.

37 If you exaggerate, you may lose credibility

The boy who cried "Wolf" is an example.

One day, as he ran through the village crying "Wolf", the wolf really was there.

But, because of the many times it wasn't, nobody believed him.

He had lost credibility.

Tell it as you see it – don't exaggerate.

If you exaggerate, you could lose credibility and it might be impossible to regain it.

38 Be careful of what you say and write

Communication with any part of the world is almost instantaneous.

Mobile phones and e-mails have changed everything.

Mobile phones have loud speakers, and emails can be forwarded immediately at the press of a button.

When speaking, assume many are listening

When writing, assume many will read.

Trust few.

We live in a litigious world and lawyers make much money as they protect their clients' interests.

Assume that whatever you say and write one day will be put to you in a court of law.

So be careful of what you say and write.

39 Avoid publicity

It is important to remember that bad news sells better than good news.

It may be a sad reflection on humanity – but that is the fact.

Those who seek publicity are often insecure.

They need to be recognised and to feel important.

They love to be photographed and written about.

They crave attention, and can't get enough of it.

Newspapers and television have made many people better known – in some instances 'famous,' and even 'heroes'.

The media have no problem in turning on the same people, when things go wrong.

You often see this in the case of footballers or politicians or show business people when there are difficulties in their private lives.

Stay out of the newspapers and off the television.

40 When time heals, don't re-open old wounds

When someone close to you dies, you feel very sad and the loss is hard to take.

But, as time goes by, you accept and you cope.

Time heals.

Similarly, many problems simply fade away as the people involved move on.

When they do, it is wise to leave them alone.

Re-opening sensitive issues can lead who knows where.

Family arguments at Christmas are an example.

Try to leave sensitive issues alone.

Let time heal – even if it takes a long time.

41 Let a big opponent punch himself out

Muhammed Ali, who was one of the world's greatest boxers faced George Foreman in a famous world heavyweight championship fight in Kinshasa.

Foreman was bigger than Ali and most people expected him to win.

Ali seemed unable to do anything but defend. He absorbed many heavy punches.

Foreman, in exasperation, punched himself out.

Then Ali beat an exhausted opponent.

Don't engage with a big adversary until you must ,no matter how great the temptation might be.

Know your strengths and be confident.

Try to avoid a battle.

But, if you must fight, fight sensibly.

Learn the lesson that Muhammed Ali taught George Foreman and the rest of the world: let a big opponent punch himself out.

42 Learn to write a short letter

One day, a manager was asked to investigate an investment.

He completed his work and handed a long report to his CEO.

Without looking at it, the CEO asked "Do we have a problem?".

The manager's response was "No".

"Why not just say that?" asked the CEO, returning the report.

As the manager was leaving, looking both pleased and puzzled, his boss said, "You have good judgement and you work hard. Take the time to write a short report".

George Bernard Shaw once apologised to a friend saying, "I wrote you a long letter, because I hadn't time to write you a short one".

It is easy to write a long letter, or report or e-mail.

It is more difficult to write short ones – and so they are not common.

When you write something, ask yourself "What does it boil down to?".

Then, just write what it boils down to.

Short letters are more effective and more appreciated.

Make the effort.

It might take longer but it is more likely to get the desired result.

43 Great meetings don't happen by chance

The Finance Director, who attended many meetings and read many reports, sent this email to the CEO and Chairman:

"If next week's meeting uses the agenda and the papers that have been circulated, in my opinion, it won't be good.

It will take too much time.

The Minutes will be queried and, after much discussion, a number of minor amendments will be agreed.

Long reports will be considered and those who prepared them congratulated, even though one or two pages on the topic would have been adequate.

Presentations will be long and full of jargon and some people won't understand them but will be afraid to ask questions.

Some will nod to convey an understanding of the IT presentation, when in fact they won't understand it.

Discussions on minor matters will occupy much time.

We won't focus enough on big and basic issues, such as sales and profits.

As there are no significant decisions to be taken, would you consider using this email as the agenda?"

The CEO and the Chairman agreed to this.

There are now fewer meetings, and reports and presentations are short – and there is a better focus on big and basic issues.

The Finance Director did himself, his colleagues and his company a good service.

The Chairman too realised that he could help to make meetings better by talking less and by allowing others to talk less, particularly on minor matters.

A great meeting requires much thought.

44 Control your weight

Your health will improve when you eliminate worry and deal with your challenges.

If you control your weight, you will give it a further boost.

The key to controlling weight is a good breakfast.

It is like putting petrol in a car before the start of the journey.

Start the day well; have a light lunch and something small in the evening.

While exercise is good for your health, it takes a lot to burn even 100 calories.

Eliminate alcohol, cakes, sweets and biscuits.

Eat only small amounts of bread, potatoes and pasta.

Eat fruit and vegetables.

Drink water.

Walk for at least 30 minutes each day.

Only eat when hungry.

45 Self-image and self-belief are important

You are breathing in a slow and shallow way through your nose and you are making each moment the best.

All the goodness is flowing in to your system.

You have good health.

You have a good sense of humour.

You have eliminated worry.

All the poison has gone from your system.

You deal well with tough situations, because your head is clear and you are positive and you are attracting good solutions.

You are kind.

You are confident.

You move at a gentle pace.

This is a good self-image. You have self-belief.

Being well-dressed, well-groomed and able to speak in public will add to your confidence.

Keeping your weight in check will help also.

You are in control.

46 You learn more over a meal than over a desk

Even though you will never really know someone, people are much more themselves over a meal. They feel more relaxed.

At a desk, they are playing a role. A desk is a barrier.

As you dine, ask your guest to talk about themselves.

Listen, listen, listen!

Observe their table manners and see whether they make their order simple or a production?

Are they at ease? How do they treat the waiter?

Ask them to order the wine.

See whether they show respect for their fellow diners.

How do they react to noise and mistakes?

Are they keen to impress? Are they insecure?

Can they make a decision? Can they come to a conclusion?

Are they a details person or a 'big picture' person?

Have they a sense of humour? Would they be a good colleague?

You can learn so much about a person over a meal!

47 Assess people on their 'home ground'

Everyone has greater strengths, weaknesses and problems than you realise.

While you will never really know someone, you will get a better understanding by meeting them in their home, which allows you to see how they live and how their spouse, their children and the dog react to them.

Observe them, too, as they play sport.

How do they react when they play well?

How do they react when they play badly?

Are they conservative? Or do they play in a 'crazy' way?

Do they indulge in gamesmanship? Do they make excuses?

Try to meet a person in a number of different settings.

Take time in making your assessment but realise that, despite your best efforts, you are wrong.

You will never have the full picture.

48 If you help, you may be ignored later – but keep helping

A friend, who was Chairman of one of Ireland's largest legal firms, told me that many clients, whom he had helped when they were in great difficulty, would later cross the street to avoid meeting him.

He believed that meeting him would have reminded them of a time that they would rather forget.

Should this happen to you, don't be hurt. Understand.

The joy that you get when helping people, in times of great difficulty for them, will be great.

Make it part of the way you live.

Do it because it is good to help another human being when he is down.

49 In times of success, beware an 'own goal'

It was a Friday afternoon in the boardroom of a bank and everyone was looking forward to the weekend.

The Credit Manager presented the last loan application of the day to the Credit Committee and it was approved.

Rather than wishing the Chairman a nice week-end and leaving, he made small talk.

He said that he had expected to be questioned more on the UK division of his client's company, as it had been going through a tough time.

The Chairman, having heard that, called for silence and reconvened the meeting.

After discussing the UK division in some depth, the loan was declined.

Once something good happens and you are pleased, say little.

Be grateful, but don't get carried away.

If you get something that you want, just say "Thank you".

Notice how often when a football team scores a goal and then celebrates, the players lose concentration and concede a goal almost immediately.

Hold your celebration until you are off-stage.

In times of success, know that the potential for an 'own goal' is high.

50 Thoughts as you begin the day

As you breathe well and decide to make each moment the best, you will fill your system with goodness and your head will be clear.

With a clear head and a positive attitude, you will be creative and you will attract many positives.

Solutions to your challenges will emerge.

Be sure to 'smell the roses'.

Be kind!

Listen!

Believe in yourself!

Keep your 'big balance sheet of life' strong.

Be grateful for the life you have.

Enjoy it!

ABOUT THE AUTHOR

Tony Spollen was educated by the Jesuits at Gonzaga College in Dublin, Ireland and later at the Institute of Chartered Accountants.

Aged 23, he was the first Financial Controller of AIIB (the merchant bank that the AIB Group, Ireland's largest bank, established in 1969 in conjunction with Hambros Bank, the Toronto Dominion Bank and Irish Life Assurance Company).

In 1986, he became Head of Internal Audit for the AIB Group.

Five years later, he left the banking sector to become an internal audit consultant, advising amongst others the European Economic & Social Committee.

He is the author of *Corporate Fraud – The Danger from Within* (Oak Tree Press, 1997).

He has served on the Boards of five State-owned organisations.

Today, he and his business partner, Detta Fanning, advise businesses on building customer numbers.

He lives in Dublin with his wife Gina, and has two daughters (Antonia and Virginia) and two sons (Garfield and Davin).

His interests are sport and reading.

OAK TREE PRESS

Oak Tree Press develops and delivers information, advice and resources for entrepreneurs and managers. It is Ireland's leading business book publisher, with an unrivalled reputation for quality titles across business, management, HR, law, marketing and enterprise topics. NuBooks is its recently-launched imprint, publishing short, focused ebooks for busy entrepreneurs and managers.

In addition, through its founder and managing director, Brian O'Kane, Oak Tree Press occupies a unique position in start-up and small business support in Ireland through its standard-setting titles, as well training courses, mentoring and advisory services.

Oak Tree Press is comfortable across a range of communication media – print, web and training, focusing always on the effective communication of business information.

Oak Tree Press, 19 Rutland Street, Cork, Ireland.
T: + 353 21 4313855 F: + 353 21 4313496.
E: info@oaktreepress.com W: www.oaktreepress.com.